foundations

SMALL GROUP STUDY

taught by tom holladay and kay warren

JESUS

 ZONDERVAN®

 SADDLEBACK CHURCH

ZONDERVAN.com/
AUTHORTRACKER
follow your favorite authors

Foundations: *Jesus Study Guide*
Copyright © 2003, 2008 by Tom Holladay and Kay Warren

Requests for information should be addressed to:
Zondervan, *Grand Rapids, Michigan 49530*

ISBN 978-0-310-27674-6

08 09 10 11 12 13 14 15 16 17 18 • 23 22 21 20 19 18 17 16 15 14 13 12 11 10 9 8 7 6 5 4 3 2 1

foundations
TABLE OF CONTENTS

Small Group Roster . . . . Inside Front Cover

Foreword *by Rick Warren* iv

Preface vi

How to Use This Video Curriculum ix

Session One: Jesus, Your Best Friend 1

Session Two: The Life of Jesus 11

Session Three: Jesus Is Fully God 21

Session Four: Jesus Is Fully God and Fully Man 33

Small Group Resources 43

    Helps for Hosts 44

    Frequently Asked Questions 48

    Group Guidelines 50

    Circles of Life Diagram 52

    Small Group Prayer and Praise Report 53

    Small Group Calendar 56

    Serving the Lord's Supper 57

    Answer Key 59

    Key Verses 61

FOREWORD

What *Foundations* Will Do for You

I once built a log cabin in the Sierra mountains of northern California. After ten backbreaking weeks of clearing forest land, all I had to show for my effort was a leveled and squared concrete foundation. I was discouraged, but my father, who built over a hundred church buildings in his lifetime, said, "Cheer up, son! Once you've laid the foundation, the most important work is behind you." I've since learned that this is a principle for all of life: you can never build *anything* larger than the foundation can handle.

The foundation of any building determines both its size and strength, and the same is true of our lives. A life built on a false or faulty foundation will never reach the height that God intends for it to reach. If you skimp on your foundation, you limit your life.

That's why this material is so vitally important. *Foundations* is the biblical basis of a purpose-driven life. You must understand these life-changing truths to enjoy God's purposes for you. This curriculum has been taught, tested, and refined over ten years with thousands of people at Saddleback Church. I've often said that *Foundations* is the most important class in our church.

Why You Need a Biblical Foundation for Life

- *It's the source of personal growth and stability.* So many of the problems in our lives are caused by faulty thinking. That's why Jesus said the truth will set us free and why Colossians 2:7a (CEV) says, *"Plant your roots in Christ and let him be the foundation for your life."*

- *It's the underpinning of a healthy family.* Proverbs 24:3 (TEV) says, *"Homes are built on the foundation of wisdom and understanding."* In a world that is constantly changing, strong families are based on God's unchanging truth.

- ***It's the starting point of leadership.*** You can never lead people farther than you've gone yourself. Proverbs 16:12b (MSG) says, *"Sound leadership has a moral foundation."*

- ***It's the basis for your eternal reward in heaven.*** Paul said, *"Whatever we build on that foundation will be tested by fire on the day of judgment . . . We will be rewarded if our building is left standing"* (1 Corinthians 3:12, 14 CEV).

- ***God's truth is the only foundation that will last.*** The Bible tells us that *"the sound, wholesome teachings of the Lord Jesus Christ . . . are the foundation for a godly life"* (1 Timothy 6:3 NLT), and that *"God's truth stands firm like a foundation stone . . . "* (2 Timothy 2:19 NLT).

Jesus concluded his Sermon on the Mount with a story illustrating this important truth. Two houses were built on different foundations. The house built on sand was destroyed when rain, floods, and wind swept it away. But the house built on the foundation of solid rock remained firm. He concluded, *"Therefore everyone who hears these words of mine and puts them into practice is like a wise man who built his house on the rock"* (Matthew 7:24 NIV). *The Message* paraphrase of this verse shows how important this is: *"These words I speak to you are not incidental additions to your life . . . They are foundational words, words to build a life on."*

I cannot recommend this curriculum more highly to you. It has changed our church, our staff, and thousands of lives. For too long, too many have thought of theology as something that doesn't relate to our everyday lives, but *Foundations* explodes that mold. This study makes it clear that the foundation of what we do and say in each day of our lives is what we believe. I am thrilled that this in-depth, life-changing curriculum is now being made available for everyone to use.

— Rick Warren, author of *The Purpose Driven® Life*

PREFACE

Get ready for a radical statement, a pronouncement sure to make you wonder if we've lost our grip on reality: *There is nothing more exciting than doctrine!*

Track with us for a second on this. Doctrine is the study of what God has to say. What God has to say is always the truth. The truth gives me the right perspective on myself and on the world around me. The right perspective results in decisions of faith and experiences of joy. *That* is exciting!

The objective of *Foundations* is to present the basic truths of the Christian faith in a simple, systematic, and life-changing way. In other words, to teach doctrine. The question is, why? In a world in which people's lives are filled with crying needs, why teach doctrine? Because biblical doctrine has the answer to many of those crying needs! Please don't see this as a clash between needs-oriented and doctrine-oriented teaching. The truth is we need both. We all need to learn how to deal with worry in our lives. One of the keys to dealing with worry is an understanding of the biblical doctrine of the hope of heaven. Couples need to know what the Bible says about how to have a better marriage. They also need a deeper understanding of the doctrine of the Fatherhood of God, giving the assurance of God's love upon which all healthy relationships are built. Parents need to understand the Bible's practical insights for raising kids. They also need an understanding of the sovereignty of God, a certainty of the fact that God is in control, that will carry them through the inevitable ups and downs of being a parent. Doctrinal truth meets our deepest needs.

Welcome to a study that will have a lifelong impact on the way that you look at everything around you and above you and within you. Helping you develop a "Christian worldview" is our goal as the writers of this study. A Christian worldview is the ability to see everything through the filter of God's truth. The time you dedicate to this study will lay a foundation for new perspectives that will have tremendous benefits for the rest of your life. This study will help you to:

- Lessen the stress in everyday life

- See the real potential for growth the Lord has given you

- Increase your sense of security in an often troubling world

- Find new tools for helping others (your friends, your family, your children) find the right perspective on life

- Fall more deeply in love with the Lord

Throughout this study you'll see three types of sidebar sections designed to help you connect with the truths God tells us about himself, ourselves, and this world.

- *A Fresh Word:* One aspect of doctrine that makes people nervous is the "big words." Throughout this study we'll take a fresh look at these words, words like *omnipotent* and *sovereign*.

- *Key Personal Perspective:* The truth of doctrine always has a profound impact on our lives. In this section we'll focus on that personal impact.

- *Living on Purpose:* James 1:22 (NCV) says, *"Do what God's teaching says; when you only listen and do nothing, you are fooling yourselves."* In his book, *The Purpose Driven Life,* Rick Warren identifies God's five purposes for our lives. They are worship, fellowship, discipleship, ministry, and evangelism. We will focus on one or two of these five purposes in each lesson, and discuss how it relates to the subject of the study. This section is very important, so please be sure to leave time for it.

Here is a brief explanation of the other features of this study guide.

Looking Ahead/Catching Up: You will open each meeting with an opportunity for everyone to check in with each other about how you are doing with the weekly assignments. Accountability is a key to success in this study!

Key Verse: Each week you will find a key verse or Scripture passage for your group to read together. If someone in the group has a different translation, ask them to read it aloud so the group can get a bigger picture of the meaning of the passage.

Video Lesson: There is a video lesson segment for the group to watch together each week. Take notes in the lesson outlines as you watch the video, and be sure to refer back to these notes during your discussion time.

Discovery Questions: Each video segment is complemented by questions for group discussion. Please don't feel pressured to discuss every single question. The material in this study is meant to be your servant, not your master, so there is no reason to rush through the answers. Give everyone ample opportunity to share their thoughts. If you don't get through all of the discovery questions, that's okay.

Prayer Direction: At the end of each session you will find suggestions for your group prayer time. Praying together is one of the greatest privileges of small group life. Please don't take it for granted.

Get ready for God to do incredible things in your life as you begin the adventure of learning more deeply about the most exciting message in the world: the truth about God!

— Tom Holladay and Kay Warren

How to Use This Video Curriculum

Here is a brief explanation of the features on your small group DVD. These features include a *Group Lifter*, four *Video Teaching Sessions* by Tom Holladay and Kay Warren, and a short video, *How to Become a Follower of Jesus Christ*, by Rick Warren. Here's how they work:

The *Group Lifter* is a brief video introduction by Tom Holladay giving you a sense of the objectives and purpose of this *Foundations* study on Jesus. Watch it together as a group at the beginning of your first session.

The *Video Teaching Sessions* provide you with the teaching for each week of the study. Watch these features with your group. After watching the video teaching session, continue in your study by working through the discussion questions and activities in the study guide.

Nothing is more important than the decision you make to accept Jesus Christ as your Lord and Savior. In Session One of this study, Kay Warren leads you in a prayer of salvation. If a member of your group is not ready to accept Christ at that time, or if you feel there is a better time to address this issue, we have included a short video presentation, *How to Become a Follower of Jesus Christ*, that you can select at the end of the session or from the Main Menu of the DVD for viewing at any time. In this video segment, Rick Warren explains in more detail the importance of having Christ as the Savior of your life and how you can become part of the family of God.

Follow these simple steps for a successful small group session:

1. Hosts: Watch the video session and write down your answers to the discussion questions in the study guide before your group arrives.

2. Group: Open your group meeting by using the "Looking Ahead" or "Catching Up" section of your lesson.

3. Group: Watch the video teaching lesson and follow along in the outlines in the study guide.

4. Group: Complete the rest of the discussion materials for each session in the study guide.

It's just that simple. Have a great study together!

1

Session One

JESUS, YOUR BEST FRIEND

LOOKING AHEAD

1. What do you hope to get out of this small group study?

2. When you think of Jesus, who do you see? Is he a friend, your Lord and Savior, someone you think is a great teacher, or just a name you occasionally hear uttered in anger? Your ideas about Jesus have doubtlessly been influenced by several factors over the course of your life. Share your thoughts about Jesus. Has he impacted your life? If so, how?

Key Verse

For in Christ all the fullness of the Deity lives in bodily form,
and you have been given fullness in Christ,
who is the head over every power and authority.

Colossians 2:9–10 (NIV)

BIBLE TEACHING

Watch the video lesson now and take notes in your outline on pages 3–5.

Why Is It Important to Know More about Jesus Christ?

How well do you know Jesus? Is he someone you know by name only? Maybe as a figure in history? Or do you count him as a friend? That's why you study the person of Jesus—so you can learn about someone who desires to be your best friend. The goal of this study is not that you will just become informed about Jesus, but that you will develop a deeper relationship with him. The more you know about him, the more you realize how deeply he loves you and how he's given you the wonderful ability to love him in return.

1. Knowing Jesus is life's continuing _____ .

    Everything else is worthless when compared with the priceless gain of knowing Christ Jesus my Lord. (Philippians 3:8a LB)

2. Knowing Jesus is the believer's continuing _____ .

    For as you know him better, he will give you, through his great power, everything you need for living a truly good life: he even shares his own glory and his own goodness with us! (2 Peter 1:3 LB)

The Names of Jesus

One of the first ways you get to know a person is by learning their name, and one of the first ways you get to know more about Jesus Christ is by learning his name. The names of Jesus help you identify who he is.

In the Bible, a name was an indicator of three specifics about a person:

_____ , _____ , _____ .

- _____ : means "salvation of God"

    You will be with child and give birth to a son, and you are to give him the name Jesus. (Luke 1:31 NIV)

    Today in the town of David a Savior has been born to you; he is Christ the Lord. (Luke 2:11 NIV)

- Savior: showing Jesus' _____
- Christ: shows Jesus' _____
- Lord: showing Jesus' _____

PRAYER OF COMMITMENT

For you to learn about Jesus without having a relationship with him would be life's greatest tragedy. If you want the kind of relationship that God made you for and Jesus died on the cross to offer you, then pray the following prayer:

Jesus Christ, today I want to begin a relationship with you.
I don't want to just know about you;
I want to know you personally.
I ask you to forgive me for the wrong things I've done.
I want to learn from you how to live.
I choose today to begin to live by your direction and guidance.
I don't even know all that will mean,
but I'm trusting in you to show me the way.
In Jesus' name. Amen.

KEY PERSONAL PERSPECTIVE

The Power of Jesus' Name

The Bible does more than just list Jesus' names; it tells us of the power of his name!

1. Jesus' name is _____ .

   ⁹Therefore God exalted him to the highest place and gave him the name that is above every name, ¹⁰that at the name of Jesus every knee should bow, in heaven and on earth and under the earth, ¹¹and every tongue confess that Jesus Christ is Lord, to the glory of God the Father.
   (Philippians 2:9–11 NIV)

2. As believers we _____ .

   - We are anointed. (James 5:14)

   - We are forgiven. (1 John 2:12)

   - We are baptized. (Acts 10:48)

   - We are justified in his name. (1 Corinthians 6:11)

   - We assemble in his name. (1 Corinthians 5:4)

   - We bear his name. (1 Peter 4:16)

   - We believe in his name. (John 1:12)

   - We call on his name. (1 Corinthians 1:2)

   - We give thanks in his name. (Ephesians 5:20)

   - We have life. (John 20:31)

   - We preach. (Acts 8:12)

   - We speak. (Acts 9:28)

   - We suffer. (Acts 21:13, 1 Peter 4:16)

   - We do everything in his name. (Colossians 3:17)

DISCOVERY QUESTIONS

1. What did you learn about Jesus today that was new, caught your attention for the first time, or was important to your belief in Jesus? What difference does this new knowledge make to you? Does it change your picture of Jesus? If so, how?

2. Which of the names of Jesus we looked at today is most meaningful to you? Why?

3. How can you balance a relationship of intimate friendship with Jesus with allowing him to be the ultimate authority in your everyday life?

4. Is the idea of a personal relationship with Jesus new to anyone in your group? Many people grow up knowing about Jesus, but never hearing they can know him personally. If anyone in your group is unsure whether or not they have this kind of relationship with Jesus, this is an ideal place to start it. Pray together the prayer of commitment on page 4 of your outline notes. First, recognize his purpose as Savior of your life and ask for his forgiveness. Second, realize his promise to us as the one sent from God. Finally, accept his position as Lord of your life.

Did You Get It? How has this week's study helped you see that there is no greater priority than your relationship with Jesus?

Share with Someone: Think of a person you can encourage with the truth you learned in this session. Write their name in the space below and pray for God to provide that opportunity this week.

LIVING ON PURPOSE

Discipleship

1. Jesus Christ wants to be your best friend. Think of it: your best friend is ruling at God's right hand. He is the one who holds everything together. This week, choose to live out and enjoy the fact that Jesus is your best friend. Here are three ways you can do that:

   · Say to yourself, "He accepts me even when I don't feel acceptable." Remind yourself throughout this week that you are Jesus' friend simply because of his grace, not because you somehow deserve that friendship.

   · Talk to him like a friend. That's what prayer is. At least once this week take a few minutes to talk to Jesus. Tell him what is happening in your life. You'll discover that talking to him about what you're facing each day, as you would to a friend, is life changing.

   · In addition to talking to him, you need to listen to him as you would your best friend. Conversation is always two-way. When we read the Bible we are reading the book he gave us. This week, listen as you read. Listen as if to the advice of a deeply trusted friend.

2. In week three of this study, you will be asked to share the story of how your relationship with Jesus began. A good way to tell this story is through the simple outline Paul used when he gave his testimony in the book of Acts.

   · My life before I came to Christ

   · How I came to know Jesus Christ

   · My life since I've come to know him

In preparation for sharing your personal Jesus story, take some time this week to write down a sentence or two about each of these three life events.

If you don't have a relationship with Jesus, consider praying the prayer on page 4 of this study guide sometime this week.

PRAYER DIRECTION

Thank God for your relationship with Jesus, specifically for the changes you've seen in your life and in the lives of those you love because of your relationship with him.

If you'd like, use the following verses as prompts for your prayers. Have someone read the verse, then let those truths direct the prayers of your group back to God.

Let your roots grow down into him and draw up nourishment from him, so you will grow in faith, strong and vigorous in the truth you were taught. Let your lives overflow with thanksgiving for all he has done. (Colossians 2:7 NLT)

[1]Since you have been raised to new life with Christ, set your sights on the realities of heaven, where Christ sits at God's right hand in the place of honor and power. [2]Let heaven fill your thoughts. Do not think only about things down here on earth. [3]For you died when Christ died, and your real life is hidden with Christ in God. [4]And when Christ, who is your real life, is revealed to the whole world, you will share in all his glory. [5]So put to death the sinful, earthly things lurking within you. Have nothing to do with sexual sin, impurity, lust, and shameful desires. Don't be greedy for the good things of this life, for that is idolatry. [6]God's terrible anger will come upon those who do such things. [7]You used to do them when your life was still part of this world. [8]But now is the time to get rid of anger, rage, malicious behavior, slander, and dirty language. [9]Don't lie to each other, for you have stripped off your old evil nature and all its wicked deeds. [10]In its place you have clothed yourselves with a brand-new nature that is continually being renewed as you learn more and more about Christ, who created this new nature within you. [11]In this new life, it doesn't matter if you are a Jew or a Gentile, circumcised or uncircumcised, barbaric, uncivilized, slave, or free. Christ is all that matters, and he lives in all of us. [12]Since God chose you to be the holy people whom he loves, you must clothe yourselves with tenderhearted mercy, kindness, humility, gentleness, and patience. [13]You must make allowance for each other's faults and forgive the person who offends you.

*Remember, the Lord forgave you, so you must forgive others.
[14]And the most important piece of clothing you must wear is
love. Love is what binds us all together in perfect harmony.
[15]And let the peace that comes from Christ rule in your hearts.
For as members of one body you are all called to live in peace.
And always be thankful. [16]Let the words of Christ, in all their
richness, live in your hearts and make you wise. Use his words
to teach and counsel each other. Sing psalms and hymns and
spiritual songs to God with thankful hearts. [17]And whatever
you do or say, let it be as a representative of the Lord Jesus, all
the while giving thanks through him to God the Father.*
(Colossians 3:1–17 NLT)

2

Session two

THE LIFE OF JESUS

CATCHING UP

1. Who did you share last week's truth with?

2. Share your experiences from this last week of acting on the truth that Jesus is our best friend. How did it go? Did you sense a new closeness and friendship with Jesus? Take a minute or two to share with the group any special insights. Did you feel any frustration, or find yourself wishing you'd remembered how close Jesus is? (Don't be afraid to share your frustrations; it will be an encouragement to others who faced the same feelings.)

Key Verse

For by him all things were created: things in heaven and on earth,
visible and invisible, whether thrones or powers or rulers or authorities;
all things were created by him and for him.

Colossians 1:16 (NIV)

tHe LIfe OF JESUS

BIBLE TEACHING

Watch the video lesson now and take notes in your outline on pages 13–17.

The Details of Jesus' Life

Jesus' life did not begin with his birth and it did not end with his death.

What Did Jesus Do before He Was Born?

Pre-incarnation refers to Jesus' _____ in heaven before he came to earth.

He has always _____ . He is eternal.

1. He _____ the universe.

> . . . all things were created by him and for him.
> Colossians 1:16 (NIV)

2. He _____ to people.

A FRESH WORD

The Angel of the Lord

A number of times in the Old Testament a figure called "the angel of the Lord" appears to people. It is evident that this is more than an angel. He is spoken of in terms that relate more to God himself. There is no single biblical reference regarding the identity of the angel of the Lord, but the great majority of Bible teachers see these as appearances of Christ on earth before his human birth. No, he did not look like Jesus of Nazareth. He did not become a man as he would when he was born in Bethlehem. He simply took on the appearance of a man.

The people Jesus ministered to as the "angel of the Lord" included:

- **Hagar:** In Genesis 16:13, Hagar recognized this angel as
  " . . . *the God who sees me . . .* " and the Bible itself refers to
  him as " . . . *the* LORD *who spoke to her . . .* " (NIV)

- **Moses:** In Exodus 3 we are told, *"²There the angel of the* LORD
  *appeared to him in flames of fire from within a bush . . . ⁴God
  called to him from within the bush, 'Moses! Moses!' "* (vv. 2, 4
  NIV)

- **Abraham:** Genesis 18:1–2 tells us that the Lord appeared to
  Abraham also in the form of a man

Jesus' Life on Earth

1. Jesus' _____

   Beginning: his birth (Matthew 1–2; Luke 1:1–2:38)
   Ending: Jesus in the temple (Luke 2:41–50)
   Significant Events:

   - Jesus' dedication at the temple (Luke 2:22–39)

   - Fleeing to Egypt (Matthew 2:13–23)

   - Jesus' visit to the temple at age twelve (Luke 2:41–50)

2. The _____ of Jesus' Life

   *And Jesus grew in wisdom and stature, and in favor with God
   and men.* (Luke 2:52 NIV)

   Significant Events:

   - His mother, Mary, was with him at his birth (Luke 2:7), at his
     death (John 19:25), to witness his resurrection, and for the
     beginning of the church on the day of Pentecost (Acts 1:14; 2:1)

   - His father, Joseph, probably died sometime after Jesus' visit to
     the temple in Jerusalem and before the beginning of his public
     ministry at age thirty

- There were at least seven children in Jesus' family: Jesus, four half brothers, and at least two half sisters (half brothers and half sisters because God was the Father of Jesus, and Joseph was the father of the others) (Matthew 13:55–56)

  - His brother Judas wrote a book in the New Testament, the book of Jude

  - His brother James also wrote one of the books in the New Testament, the book of James. He also became a leader in the Jerusalem church (Acts 12:17; 15:13–21)

3. Beginning of Jesus' _____

   Significant Events:

   - The ministry of John the Baptist (Mark 1:1–8; Luke 3:1–18)

   - Jesus' baptism (Matthew 3:13–17; Mark 1:9–11)

   - Jesus' temptation in the wilderness (Luke 4:1–13; Matthew 4:1–11)

   - Jesus' turning the water to wine (John 2:1–11)

4. Jesus' Ministry in _____

   Beginning: Cleansing the temple (John 2:13–16)
   Ending: Conversation with the woman at the well (John 4:1–42)
   Significant Event:

   - Conversation with Nicodemus (John 3:1–21)

5. Jesus' Ministry in _____

   Beginning: Healing a nobleman's son at Capernaum (John 4:46–53)
   Ending:

   - Peter's statement of trust (Matthew 16:13–20)

   - Jesus' transfiguration (Matthew 17:1–13; Luke 9:28–36)

Significant Events:

- Sermon on the Mount (Matthew 5–7)
- Calling of the disciples (Luke 5:1–11; Mark 2:13–14; Luke 6:12–16)
- Feeding of the 5,000 (Matthew 14:13–21; Mark 6:30–44)

6. Jesus' Journey to _____

> . . . *Jesus resolutely set out for Jerusalem.* (Luke 9:51 NIV)

> . . . *He resolutely set His face to go to Jerusalem . . .* (Luke 9:51 NASB)

Beginning: Jesus sets out for Jerusalem (Luke 9:51)
Ending: Mary's anointing of his body for burial (John 12:1–8)
Significant Events:

- Clashes with the Pharisees (Luke 14; Luke 16:14–15)
- The resurrection of Lazarus (John 11:1–44)
- Meets Zacchaeus in Jericho (Luke 19:1–10)

7. Jesus' Death, Burial, and _____

Beginning: His triumphal entry into Jerusalem (Mark 11:1–11)
Ending: His ascension into heaven (Luke 24:50–53)
Significant Events:

- Cleansing the temple, the Garden of Gethsemane, trials (Luke 19:45–46; John 17–18)
- Jesus' death on the cross (Matthew 27:31–50; Luke 23:26–46)
- Jesus' burial (Mark 15:42–47; John 19:38–42)
- Jesus' resurrection (Matthew 28:2–15; Mark 16:1–17; Luke 24:1–7; John 20:1–18)

> ## KEY PERSONAL PERSPECTIVE
> ### *The Historical Jesus*
>
> Jesus is a part of history. In the *Encyclopedia Britannica*, following a discussion of the writings about Jesus outside of the New Testament, the following statement is made: "These independent accounts prove that in ancient times even the opponents of Christianity never doubted the historicity of Jesus, which was disputed for the first time and on inadequate grounds by several authors at the end of the 18th, during the 19th and at the beginning of the 20th centuries."[1]
>
> *For God so loved the world that he gave his one and only Son, that whoever believes in him shall not perish but have eternal life.*
> (John 3:16 NIV)

The Eternally Existent Christ

1. What does he look like?

   - Jesus _____ in his resurrected body (Luke 24:50–53)

   - Jesus will _____ in his resurrected body (Acts 1:9–11)

2. What is he doing in heaven?

   - He is _____at God's right hand (Ephesians 1:20–22; 1 Peter 3:22)

   - He is _____ for us (Romans 8:34)

   - He is holding the _____together (Colossians 1:16–17)

   - He is anxiously _____ for us to be with him (John 14:1–3; John 17:24)

---

[1] *Encyclopedia Britannica*, 15th ed., s.v. "Jesus Christ."

DISCOVERY QUESTIONS

1. When you get to heaven and come face to face with the eternally existent Jesus:

   • What do you want to say to him?

   • What question do you most want to ask him?

   • What emotions do you think you'll experience?

2. Our teaching in this session reviewed some of the events of Jesus' earthly life. Share one episode that is most significant to you. What makes this event so meaningful?

3. We looked at several aspects of what Jesus is doing now, in heaven with the Father, where he is waiting to return. Which stands out as most important to you? (See page 17 of your outline notes.)

Did You Get It? How has this week's study helped you see, in the events of Jesus' life, some encouragement or inspiration for your daily life?

Share with Someone: Think of a person you can encourage with the truth you learned in this session. Write their name in the space below and pray for God to provide that opportunity this week.

LIVING ON PURPOSE
Ministry

1. Jesus' love for people is a quality of his life that jumps off the pages of the Bible. His life was all about serving others. Even before he gave his life on the cross, he gave himself to individuals daily. Repeatedly the Bible says he was filled with compassion for the crowds he saw. Jesus is our example of how to relate to others.

   Those who get close to him end up being more and more like him, wanting to serve others as he did. Who needs your service in Jesus' name this next week? It doesn't have to be something big or noticeable. In Matthew 10:42, Jesus says, *"And if anyone gives even a cup of cold water to one of these little ones because he is my disciple, I tell you the truth, he will certainly not lose his reward"* (NIV).

   From now on, look for ways to do little acts of ministry in Jesus' name. You don't need to announce his presence: "I'm unselfishly bringing you this cup of coffee, in the name of my Lord and Savior Jesus Christ!" Just do it—without calling attention to yourself.

   Make this a group exercise! As a group, commit to meeting the needs of someone this week. This could be someone in the group or outside the group. Is there a single parent in the group who is struggling with the burden of daily tasks? Could he or she use your assistance? Could you bring a meal to someone having health difficulties? Is there someone you know at church who has a need you could help meet? Choose one person and make a plan to help him or her in some way this week.

2. Last week you started writing the story of your relationship with Jesus. This week, take time to complete it. In order for the story to be brief enough to (a) remember, and (b) tell someone else, write down only a paragraph or two on the three subjects we looked at last week.

   · My life before I came to Christ
   · How I came to know Jesus Christ
   · My life since I've come to know him

PRAYER DIRECTION

Take some time as a group to talk about specific prayer requests, and to pray for one another.

3

Session three

JESUS IS FULLY GOD

CATCHING UP

1. Who did you share last week's truth with?

2. As your group ministered to meet someone's practical need this last week, what did you learn together?

Key Verse

In the beginning was the Word,
and the Word was with God,
and the Word was God.

John 1:1 (NIV)

BIBLE TEACHING
Watch the video lesson now and take notes in your outline on pages 23–28.

What Does It Mean When We Say that Jesus Is Both Man and God?

Is Jesus . . .

- A man who became God?

- God indwelling a man?

- God appearing to be a man?

- A spiritual being ordered by God to become man?

- Fully God and fully man?

> *In the beginning was the Word, and the Word was with God, and the Word was God.* (John 1:1 NIV)

> *. . . anyone who acknowledges that Jesus Christ came as a human being has the Spirit who comes from God.* (1 John 4:2 GNT)

Jesus Is God

How Do We Know Jesus is God?

1. _____ said he is God.

> *. . . he was even calling God his own Father, making himself equal with God.* (John 5:18 NIV)

"I and the Father are one." (John 10:30 NIV)

" . . . Anyone who has seen me has seen the Father . . . "
(John 14:9 NIV)

"I tell you the truth," Jesus answered, "before Abraham was born, I am!" (John 8:58 NIV)

2. _____ said he is God.

This started in the prophecies of Jesus' birth before he was born.

. . . And he will be called . . . Mighty God . . . (Isaiah 9:6 NIV)

It continued with those who were closest to him, his own disciples.

[10]So that at the name of Jesus every knee will bow . . . [11]and that every tongue will confess that Jesus Christ is Lord . . . (Philippians 2:10–11 NASB)

Compare Philippians 2:10–11 with what is said of God in Isaiah.

[22] . . . I am God, and there is no other . . . [23]before me every knee will bow; by me every tongue will swear. (Isaiah 45:22–23 NIV)

For in Christ all the fullness of the Deity lives in bodily form . . . (Colossians 2:9 NIV)

[1]In the beginning was the Word, and the Word was with God, and the Word was God. [2]He was with God in the beginning. (John 1:1–2 NIV)

3. He is _____ as God.

- Many worshiped him: a healed leper (Matthew 8:2), women (Matthew 15:25), the mother of James and John (Matthew 20:20), a Gerasenes demoniac (Mark 5:6), a blind man (John 9:3)

- He accepted such worship (John 20:28–29; Matthew 14:33; 28:9–10)

- His disciples prayed to him (Acts 7:59)

4. He does what only _____ can do.

- He has the power to forgive sins (Mark 2:1–12)

- All judgment is in his hands (John 5:27; Acts 17:31)

- He sends the Spirit (John 15:26)

- He will raise the dead (John 5:25)

- He is the Creator (John 1:3; Colossians 1:16; Hebrews 1:10)

- He is the Sustainer, upholding all (Colossians 1:17; Hebrews 1:3)

What Evidence Supports Jesus' Claim to Be God?

Evidence #1: The _____ of Prophecy

> *He said to them, "This is what I told you while I was still with you: Everything must be fulfilled that is written about me in the Law of Moses, the Prophets and the Psalms."*
> (Luke 24:44 NIV)

FULFILLED PROPHECY

Old Testament verses are the prophecy. The New Testament verses proclaim the fulfillment.

1. Born of a virgin (Isaiah 7:14; Matthew 1:21–23)

2. A descendent of Abraham (Genesis 12:1–3; 22:18; Matthew 1:1; Galatians 3:16)

3. Of the tribe of Judah (Genesis 49:10; Luke 3:23, 33; Hebrews 7:14)

4. Of the house of David (2 Samuel 7:12–16; Matthew 1:1)

5. Born in Bethlehem (Micah 5:2; Matthew 2:1; Luke 2:4–7)

6. Taken to Egypt (Hosea 11:1; Matthew 2:14–15)

7. Herod's killing of the infants (Jeremiah 31:15; Matthew 2:16–18)

8. Anointed by the Holy Spirit (Isaiah 11:2; Matthew 3:16–17)

9. Heralded by the messenger of the Lord (John the Baptist) (Isaiah 40:3; Malachi 3:1; Matthew 3:1–3)

10. Would perform miracles (Isaiah 35:5–6; Matthew 9:35)

11. Would preach good news (Isaiah 61:1; Luke 4:14–21)

12. Would minister in Galilee (Isaiah 9:1; Matthew 4:12–16)

13. Would cleanse the temple (Malachi 3:1, 3; Matthew 21:12–13)

14. Would enter Jerusalem as a king on a donkey (Zechariah 9:9; Matthew 21:4–9)

15. Would be rejected by Jews (Psalm 118:22; 1 Peter 2:7)

16. Would die a humiliating death (Psalm 22; Isaiah 53) involving:

    - rejection (Isaiah 53:3; John 1:10–11; 7:5, 48)

    - betrayal by a friend (Psalm 41:9; Luke 22:3–4; John 13:18)

    - being sold for thirty pieces of silver (Zechariah 11:12; Matthew 26:14–15)

    - silence before his accusers (Isaiah 53:7; Matthew 27:12–14)

    - being mocked (Psalm 22:7–8; Matthew 27:31)

    - being beaten (Isaiah 52:14; Matthew 27:26)

    - being spit upon (Isaiah 50:6; Matthew 27:30)

    - piercing his hands and feet (Psalm 22:16; Matthew 27:31)

    - being crucified with thieves (Isaiah 53:12; Matthew 27:38)

    - praying for his persecutors (Isaiah 53:12; Luke 23:34)

    - piercing his side (Zechariah 12:10; John 19:34)

    - being given gall and vinegar to drink (Psalm 69:21; Matthew 27:34; Luke 23:36)

    - no broken bones (Psalm 34:20; John 19:32–36)

    - being buried in a rich man's tomb (Isaiah 53:9; Matthew 27:57–60)

    - casting lots for his garments (Psalm 22:18; John 19:23–24)

17. Would rise from the dead (Psalm 16:10; Mark 16:6; Acts 2:31)

18. Would ascend into heaven (Psalm 68:18; Acts 1:9)

19. Would sit down at the right hand of God (Psalm 110:1; Hebrews 1:3)

These predictions were more than just a matter of chance. Some of these fulfillments of prophecy are beyond any statistical probability because they took the power of God in the fulfillment.

Evidence #2: His _____

> . . . *"Go back and report to John what you have seen and heard: The blind receive sight, the lame walk, those who have leprosy are cured, the deaf hear, the dead are raised, and the good news is preached to the poor."* (Luke 7:22 NIV)

"The blind receive sight" (Matthew 9:27–31; Luke 18:35–43; Mark 8:22–26)

"The lame walk" (Matthew 9:2–7)

"Those who have leprosy are cured" (Matthew 8:2–3; Luke 17:11–19)

"The deaf hear" (Mark 7:31–37)

"The dead are raised" (Matthew 9:18–19, 23–25; Luke 7:11–15; John 11:1–44)

"The good news is preached" (Matthew 11:5)

Evidence #3: His _____

1. Jesus not only predicted it but told the number of days!

> *Jesus answered them, "Destroy this temple, and I will raise it again in three days."* (John 2:19 NIV)

> *"For as Jonah was three days and three nights in the belly of a huge fish, so the Son of Man will be three days and three nights in the heart of the earth."* (Matthew 12:40 NIV)

> *He then began to teach them that the Son of Man must suffer many things and be rejected by the elders, chief priests and teachers of the law, and that he must be killed and after three days rise again.* (Mark 8:31 NIV)

2. Jesus claimed the _____ behind the resurrection.

> [17] "The reason my Father loves me is that I lay down my life—only to take it up again. [18] No one takes it from me, but I lay it down of my own accord. I have authority to lay it down and authority to take it up again. This command I received from my Father." (John 10:17–18 NIV)

DISCOVERY QUESTIONS

1. Do you find it difficult to believe that Jesus is fully God? Why or why not?

2. Which of the evidences you heard today regarding Jesus being fully God was most helpful to you in understanding this important doctrine? Why does this evidence matter to you?

3. How does the truth that Jesus is fully God give you a sense of confidence and security in your everyday life?

4. Even with the overwhelming proof that Jesus is fully God, many people struggle to believe it. What's the difference between physical proof and personal faith? Is faith something we should have without any proof at all? Is proof a guarantee we will have faith? Why or why not?

Did You Get It? How has this week's study helped you see that you can trust Jesus' word about who he says he is?

Share with Someone: Think of a person you can encourage with the truth you learned in this session. Write their name in the space below and pray for God to provide that opportunity this week.

LIVING ON PURPOSE
Evangelism

1. Over the last two weeks, you have written your story of your personal relationship with Jesus. Pair up with someone in the group and share your stories with each other. If time allows, share these with the whole group. If there is not time for everyone to share, consider hearing from two to three people each week until you have heard everyone's stories.

2. Now that you are more confident sharing your story, think of someone you know with whom you can share it this week. Write that person's name below and begin praying for an opportunity to share with them.

Name: _____

PRAYER DIRECTION

Take a few minutes to thank God for making it possible to know Jesus as our best friend. In short, one-sentence prayers, thank God for each proof of Jesus' deity, and its importance to your relationship with him. (*Examples:* his fulfillment of prophecy, his miracles, or his resurrection.)

Preparation for next time: For next week's *Living on Purpose* activity you will share the Lord's Supper together as a group. The Lord's Supper is an expression of participating in the life and death of Jesus Christ. When we share this experience together we worship our Lord for coming, dying, and providing the opportunity for eternal life. Take a few moments now to plan this time of communion. Turn to page 57 in the Small Group Resources section for instructions.

NOTES

Session four

4

JESUS IS FULLY GOD
AND FULLY MAN

CATCHING UP

Who did you share last week's truth with? What did you learn during last week's purpose activity?

Key Verse

Your attitude should be the same as that of Christ Jesus.

Philippians 2:5 (NIV)

BIBLE TEACHING
Watch the video lesson now and take notes in your outline on pages 33–36.

Jesus Is Man

How Do We Know that Jesus Is Man?

1. He had a _____ . (Isaiah 7:14–16; Matthew 1:23; Galatians 4:4)

2. He showed human _____ .

> *And Jesus grew in wisdom and stature, and in favor with God and men.* (Luke 2:52 NIV)

Jesus grew . . . (Luke 2:40, 52)

- _____
- _____
- _____
- _____

3. He experienced _____ .

Jesus felt . . .

- Grief (John 11:35)
- Sorrow (Matthew 26:38)
- Amazement (Matthew 8:10)
- Love
  - for an unbeliever (Mark 10:21)
  - for his friends (John 11:5)
  - for his disciples (John 13:1)
  - for his mother (John 19:26–27)
- Wonder (Mark 6:6)
- Distress (Mark 14:33)
- Compassion (Mark 1:41)
- Anger (Mark 3:5)

4. He had human _____ and _____ .

- He was tired (John 4:6; Mark 4:38)
- He was hungry (Matthew 4:2)
- He was thirsty (John 19:28)
- He was in agony (Luke 22:44)
- He was tempted (Matthew 4:1–11)
- He died (Luke 23:46)

> **A FRESH WORD**
>
> ## Incarnation
>
> The word *incarnation* is from the Latin for "in the flesh." When Jesus was born in Bethlehem, it was the incarnation of God into this world. God came to us in human flesh.

The Dual Nature of Jesus Christ

Jesus Is Fully God and Fully Man

The council of Chalcedon was a group called together in 451 AD to deal with false teaching in that day as to the nature of Jesus. In their famous affirmation of the truth that Jesus is fully God and fully man, they wrote that Jesus existed "in two natures which exist without confusion, without change, without division, without separation, the difference of the natures having been in no wise taken away by reason of the union, but rather the properties of each being preserved, and both concurring in one person."

Jesus is perfect humanity wrapped around undiminished deity. The theological term for this is hypostatic union.

> **A FRESH WORD**
>
> ## Hypostatic Union
>
> The union of undiminished deity and perfect humanity forever in one person. That means that Jesus not only became God and man but that he will always be God and man.
>
> 1. Jesus always has been God (John 1:2).
>
> 2. Jesus became man while continuing to be God (John 1:14).
>
> 3. Jesus continues to exist as God and man (Acts 1:9–11).

While Jesus was in this world he made a choice:

1. Jesus _____ himself.

   Four ways that Jesus limited himself:

   - He took the form of a man (Philippians 2:6–8)
   - He limited his presence to one place and one time
   - He took a position in which the Father was "greater" (John 14:28)
   - He limited his understanding (Matthew 24:36)

2. Jesus did not _____ himself.

   - He was still fully God as he walked this earth (Mark 2:8; Matthew 26:53)
   - The decision to be born a man, to walk this earth, and to die on a cross was made for him as a part of the Trinity
   - This attitude is _____
     (Philippians 2:3–4)
     - As fully man, Jesus shows us that he _____ our needs
     - As fully God, Jesus shows us that he can _____ our needs

DISCOVERY QUESTIONS

1. Which is harder for you to see as real: the fact that Jesus is completely God or the fact that Jesus is completely man?

2. We know Jesus can identify with our struggles and weaknesses because he became a person. Right now, where are you most glad he is able to identify with you? Talk about one or two areas that are especially meaningful to you.

   - Tiredness
   - Disappointment
   - Stress
   - Temptations
   - Betrayal
   - Emotions
   - Relationships

3. How has this study helped you fix your eyes on Jesus and become better friends with him?

4. What does humility look like in our daily lives? When and how can we be like Jesus by willingly putting others ahead of ourselves? Discuss examples.

5. As you end this study, look at three ways to begin to act this next week on the truth that Jesus is your best friend: remind yourself of his acceptance of you as a friend, talk to him as a friend, or listen to him as a friend. Which of these do you think would best help you come to a new understanding and appreciation of your friendship with Jesus? Why?

Did You Get It? How has this week's study helped you see Jesus in a more personal way?

Share with Someone: Think of a person you can encourage with the truth you learned in this session. Write their name in the space below and pray for God to provide that opportunity this week.

LIVING ON PURPOSE

Evangelism

Continue sharing your group members' stories as you began to do last week. If there is not enough time for everyone to finish sharing, continue hearing from a couple of people each time you get together until you have heard from everyone.

LIVING ON PURPOSE

Worship

One of the most effective ways to finish this study would be to share the Lord's Supper together as a group. (See page 57 in the Small Group Resources section.) Christ's sacrifice on the cross is a wonderful example of his commitment to being your best friend. Enjoy the Lord's Supper as a group and close your time by expressing praise and thanks to God.

PRAYER DIRECTION

Take some time as a group to talk about specific prayer requests, and to pray for one another.

NOTES

SMALL GROUP RESOURCES

HELPS FOR HOSTS

Top Ten Ideas for New Hosts

Congratulations! As the host of your small group, you have responded to the call to help shepherd Jesus' flock. Few other tasks in the family of God surpass the contribution you will be making.

As you prepare to facilitate your group, whether it is one session or the entire series, here are a few thoughts to keep in mind. We encourage you to read and review these tips with each new discussion host before he or she leads.

Remember you are not alone. God knows everything about you, and he knew you would be asked to facilitate your group. Even though you may not feel ready, this is common for all good hosts. God promises, *"I will never leave you; I will never abandon you"* (Hebrews 13:5 TEV). Whether you are facilitating for one evening, several weeks, or a lifetime, you will be blessed as you serve.

1. **Don't try to do it alone.** Pray right now for God to help you build a healthy team. If you can enlist a cohost to help you shepherd the group, you will find your experience much richer. This is your chance to involve as many people as you can in building a healthy group. All you have to do is ask people to help. You'll be surprised at the response.

2. **Be friendly and be yourself.** God wants to use your unique gifts and temperament. Be sure to greet people at the door with a big smile . . . this can set the mood for the whole gathering. Remember, they are taking as big a step to show up at your house as you are to lead this group! Don't try to do things exactly like another host; do them in a way that fits you. Admit when you don't have an answer and apologize when you make a mistake. Your group will love you for it and you'll sleep better at night.

3. **Prepare for your meeting ahead of time.** Review the session and write down your responses to each question. Pay special attention to exercises that ask group members to do something other than engage in discussion. These exercises will help your group live what the Bible teaches, not just talk about it. Be sure you understand how an exercise works. If the exercise employs one of the items in the Small Group Resources section (such as the Group Guidelines), be sure to look over that item so you'll know how it works.

4. **Pray for your group members by name.** Before you begin your session, take a few moments and pray for each member by name. You may want to review the prayer list at least once a week. Ask God to use your time together to touch the heart of every person in your group. Expect God to lead you to whomever he wants you to encourage or challenge in a special way. If you listen, God will surely lead.

5. **When you ask a question, be patient.** Someone will eventually respond. Sometimes people need a moment or two of silence to think about the question. If silence doesn't bother you, it won't bother anyone else. After someone responds, affirm the response with a simple "thanks" or "great answer." Then ask, "How about somebody else?" or "Would someone who hasn't shared like to add anything?" Be sensitive to new people or reluctant members who aren't ready to say, pray, or do anything. If you give them a safe setting, they will blossom over time. If someone in your group is a "wallflower" who sits silently through every session, consider talking to them privately and encouraging them to participate. Let them know how important they are to you—that they are loved and appreciated—and that the group would value their input. Remember, still water often runs deep.

6. **Provide transitions between questions.** Ask if anyone would like to read the paragraph or Bible passage. Don't call on anyone, but ask for a volunteer, and then be patient until someone begins. Be sure to thank the person who reads aloud.

7. **Break into smaller groups occasionally.** With a greater opportunity to talk in a small circle, people will connect more with the study, apply more quickly what they're learning, and ultimately get more out of their small group experience. A small circle also encourages a quiet person to participate and tends to minimize the effects of a more vocal or dominant member.

8. **Small circles are also helpful during prayer time.** People who are unaccustomed to praying aloud will feel more comfortable trying it with just two or three others. Also, prayer requests won't take as much time, so circles will have more time to actually pray. When you gather back with the whole group, you can have one person from each circle briefly update everyone on the prayer requests from their subgroups. The other great aspect of subgrouping is that it fosters leadership development. As you ask people in the group to facilitate discussion or to lead a prayer circle, it gives them a small leadership step that can build their confidence.

9. **Rotate facilitators occasionally.** You may be perfectly capable of hosting each time, but you will help others grow in their faith and gifts if you give them opportunities to host the group.

10. **One final challenge (for new or first-time hosts).** Before your first opportunity to lead, look up each of the six passages that follow. Read each one as a devotional exercise to help prepare you with a shepherd's heart. Trust us on this one. If you do this, you will be more than ready for your first meeting.

Matthew 9:36–38 (NIV)
36When Jesus saw the crowds, he had compassion on them, because they were harassed and helpless, like sheep without a shepherd. 37Then he said to his disciples, "The harvest is plentiful but the workers are few. 38Ask the Lord of the harvest, therefore, to send out workers into his harvest field."

John 10:14–15 (NIV)
14I am the good shepherd; I know my sheep and my sheep know me—15just as the Father knows me and I know the Father—and I lay down my life for the sheep.

1 Peter 5:2–4 (NIV)

²Be shepherds of God's flock that is under your care, serving as overseers—not because you must, but because you are willing, as God wants you to be; ³not greedy for money, but eager to serve; not lording it over those entrusted to you, but being examples to the flock. ⁴And when the Chief Shepherd appears, you will receive the crown of glory that will never fade away.

Philippians 2:1–5 (NIV)

¹If you have any encouragement from being united with Christ, if any comfort from his love, if any fellowship with the Spirit, if any tenderness and compassion, ²then make my joy complete by being like-minded, having the same love, being one in spirit and purpose. ³Do nothing out of selfish ambition or vain conceit, but in humility consider others better than yourselves. ⁴Each of you should look not only to your own interests, but also to the interests of others. ⁵Your attitude should be the same as that of Jesus Christ.

Hebrews 10:23–25 (NIV)

²³Let us hold unswervingly to the hope we profess, for he who promised is faithful. ²⁴And let us consider how we may spur one another on toward love and good deeds. ²⁵Let us not give up meeting together, as some are in the habit of doing, but let us encourage one another—and all the more as you see the Day approaching.

1 Thessalonians 2:7–8, 11–12 (NIV)

⁷. . . but we were gentle among you, like a mother caring for her little children. ⁸We loved you so much that we were delighted to share with you not only the gospel of God but our lives as well, because you had become so dear to us. . . . ¹¹For you know that we dealt with each of you as a father deals with his own children, ¹²encouraging, comforting and urging you to live lives worthy of God, who calls you into his kingdom and glory.

FREQUENTLY ASKED QUESTIONS

How long will this group meet?

This volume of *Foundations: Jesus* is four sessions long. We encourage your group to add a fifth session for a celebration. In your final session, each group member may decide if he or she desires to continue on for another study. At that time you may also want to do some informal evaluation, discuss your Group Guidelines, and decide which study you want to do next. We recommend you visit our website at **www.saddlebackresources.com** for more video-based small group studies.

Who is the host?

The host is the person who coordinates and facilitates your group meetings. In addition to a host, we encourage you to select one or more group members to lead your group discussions. Several other responsibilities can be rotated, including refreshments, prayer requests, worship, or keeping up with those who miss a meeting. Shared ownership in the group helps everybody grow.

Where do we find new group members?

Recruiting new members can be a challenge for groups, especially new groups with just a few people, or existing groups that lose a few people along the way. We encourage you to use the *Circles of Life* diagram on page 52 of this DVD study guide to brainstorm a list of people from your workplace, church, school, neighborhood, family, and so on. Then pray for the people on each member's list. Allow each member to invite several people from their list. Some groups fear that newcomers will interrupt the intimacy that members have built over time. However, groups that welcome newcomers generally gain strength with the infusion of new blood. Remember, the next person you add just might become a friend for eternity. Logistically, groups find different ways to add members. Some groups remain permanently open, while others choose to open periodically, such as at the beginning or end of a study. If your group becomes too large for easy, face-to-face conversations, you can subgroup, forming a second discussion group in another room.

How do we handle the child care needs in our group?

Child care needs must be handled very carefully. This is a sensitive issue. We suggest you seek creative solutions as a group. One common solution is to have the adults meet in the living room and share the cost of a babysitter (or two) who can be with the kids in another part of the house. Another popular option is to have one home for the kids (supervised, of course) and a second home (close by) for the adults. If desired, the adults could rotate the responsibility of providing a lesson for the kids. This last option is great with school-age kids and can be a huge blessing to families.

GROUP GUIDELINES

It's a good idea for every group to put words to their shared values, expectations, and commitments. Such guidelines will help you avoid unspoken agendas and unmet expectations. We recommend you discuss your guidelines during Session One in order to lay the foundation for a healthy group experience. Feel free to modify anything that does not work for your group.

We agree to the following values:

Clear Purpose	To grow healthy spiritual lives by building a healthy small group community
Group Attendance	To give priority to the group meeting (call if I am absent or late)
Safe Environment	To create a safe place where people can be heard and feel loved (no quick answers, snap judgments, or simple fixes)
Be Confidential	To keep anything that is shared strictly confidential and within the group
Conflict Resolution	To avoid gossip and to immediately resolve any concerns by following the principles of Matthew 18:15–17
Spiritual Health	To give group members permission to speak into my life and help me live a healthy, balanced spiritual life that is pleasing to God
Limit Our Freedom	To limit our freedom by not serving or consuming alcohol during small group meetings or events so as to avoid causing a weaker brother or sister to stumble (1 Corinthians 8:1–13; Romans 14:19–21)

Welcome Newcomers   To invite friends who might benefit from this study and warmly welcome newcomers

Building Relationships   To get to know the other members of the group and pray for them regularly

Other   _____

We have also discussed and agreed on the following items:

Child Care

_____

_____

Starting Time

_____

Ending Time

_____

If you haven't already done so, take a few minutes to fill out the *Small Group Calendar* on page 56.

CIRCLES OF LIFE—SMALL GROUP CONNECTIONS

Discover who you can connect in community

Use this chart to help carry out one of the values in the Group Guidelines to "Welcome Newcomers."

"Follow me, and I will make you fishers of men." (Matthew 4:19 KJV)

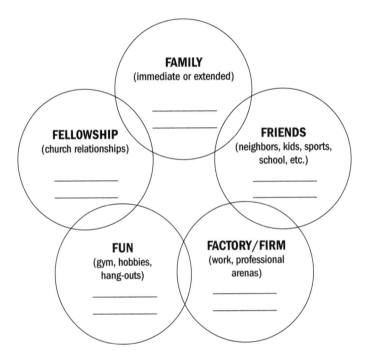

Follow this simple three-step process:

1. List 1–2 people in each circle.

2. Prayerfully select one person or couple from your list and tell your group about them.

3. Give them a call and invite them to your next meeting. Over 50 percent of those invited to a small group say, "Yes!"

SMALL GROUP PRAYER AND PRAISE REPORT

This is a place where you can write each other's requests for prayer. You can also make a note when God answers a prayer. Pray for each other's requests. If you're new to group prayer, it's okay to pray silently or to pray by using just one sentence: "God, please help

_____ to _____."

DATE	PERSON	PRAYER REQUEST	PRAISE REPORT

SMALL GROUP PRAYER AND PRAISE REPORT

DATE	PERSON	PRAYER REQUEST	PRAISE REPORT

SMALL GROUP PRAYER AND PRAISE REPORT

DATE	PERSON	PRAYER REQUEST	PRAISE REPORT

SMALL GROUP CALENDAR

Healthy groups share responsibilities and group ownership. It might take some time for this to develop. Shared ownership ensures that responsibility for the group doesn't fall to one person. Use the calendar to keep track of social events, mission projects, birthdays, or days off. Complete this calendar at your first or second meeting. Planning ahead will increase attendance and shared ownership.

DATE	LESSON	LOCATION	FACILITATOR	SNACK OR MEAL
5/4	Session 2	Chris and Andrea	Jim Brown	Phil and Karen

SERVING THE LORD'S SUPPER

[23] . . . The Lord Jesus, on the night he was betrayed, took bread, [24]and when he had given thanks, he broke it and said, "This is my body, which is for you; do this in remembrance of me." [25]In the same way, after supper he took the cup, saying, "This cup is the new covenant in my blood; do this, whenever you drink it, in remembrance of me." [26]For whenever you eat this bread and drink this cup, you proclaim the Lord's death until he comes. (1 Corinthians 11:23–26 NIV)

Steps in Serving Communion

(Before serving communion in your small group, check with your pastor and church leadership to be sure that serving communion in a small group fits the practice and philosophy of your church.)

1. Open by sharing about God's love, forgiveness, grace, mercy, commitment, tenderheartedness, faithfulness, etc., out of your personal journey (connect with stories of those in the room).

2. Read the passage: *. . . The Lord Jesus, on the night he was betrayed, took bread, and when he had given thanks, he broke it and said, "This is my body, which is for you; do this in remembrance of me."* (vv. 23–24)

3. Pray and pass the bread around the circle (could be time for quiet reflection, singing a simple praise song, or listening to a worship tape).

4. When everyone has been served, remind him or her that this represents Jesus' body broken on their behalf. Simply state, "Jesus said, 'Do this in remembrance of me.' Let us eat together," and eat the bread as a group.

5. Then read the rest of the passage: *In the same way, after supper he took the cup, saying, "This cup is the new covenant in my blood; do this, whenever you drink it, in remembrance of me."* (v. 25)

6. Pray and serve the cups, either by passing a small tray, serving them individually, or having members pick up a cup from the table.

7. When everyone has been served, remind them the juice represents Christ's blood shed for them, then simply state, "Take and drink in remembrance of him. Let us drink together."

8. Finish by singing a simple song, listening to a praise song, or having a time of prayer in thanks to God.

Several Practical Tips in Serving Communion

1. Be sensitive to timing in your meeting.

2. Break up pieces of cracker or soft bread on a small plate or tray. Don't use large servings of bread or juice.

3. Prepare all of the elements beforehand and bring these into the room when you are ready.

Communion passages: Matthew 26:26–29; Mark 14:22–25; Luke 22:14–20; 1 Corinthians 10:16–21, 11:17–34

ANSWER KEY

Session One: Jesus, Your Best Friend

1. Knowing Jesus is life's continuing <u>priority</u>.

2. Knowing Jesus is the believer's continuing <u>challenge</u>.

In the Bible, a name was an indicator of three specifics about a person: <u>his purpose, his promise, his position</u>.

- Jesus: means "salvation of God"
- Savior: showing Jesus' <u>purpose</u>
- Christ: shows Jesus' <u>promise</u>
- Lord: showing Jesus' <u>position</u>

1. Jesus' name is <u>above all names</u>.

2. As believers we <u>live in his name</u>.

Session Two: The Life of Jesus

Pre-incarnation refers to Jesus' <u>existence</u> in heaven before he came to earth.

He has always <u>existed</u>. He is eternal.

1. He <u>created</u> the universe.

2. He <u>ministered</u> to people.

1. Jesus' <u>Boyhood</u>

2. The <u>Silent Years</u> of Jesus' Life

3. Beginning of Jesus' <u>Ministry</u>

4. Jesus' Ministry in <u>Judea</u>

5. Jesus' Ministry in <u>Galilee</u>

6. Jesus' Journey to <u>Jerusalem</u>

7. Jesus' Death, Burial, and <u>Resurrection</u>

- Jesus <u>exists</u> in his resurrected body
- Jesus will <u>return</u> in his resurrected body
- He is <u>ruling</u> at God's right hand
- He is <u>praying</u> for us
- He is holding the <u>universe</u> together
- He is anxiously <u>waiting</u> for us to be with him

Session Three: Jesus Is Fully God

1. <u>Jesus</u> said he is God.

2. <u>Others</u> said he is God.

3. He is <u>worshiped</u> as God.

4. He does what only <u>God</u> can do.

Evidence #1: The <u>Fulfillment</u> of Prophecy

Evidence #2: His <u>Miracles</u>

Evidence #3: His <u>Resurrection</u>

2. Jesus claimed the <u>authority</u> behind the resurrection.

Session Four: Jesus Is Fully God and Fully Man

1. He had a <u>human birth</u>.

2. He showed human <u>growth</u>.
   Jesus grew:
   - <u>intellectually</u>
   - <u>physically</u>
   - <u>spiritually</u>
   - <u>socially</u>

3. He experienced <u>emotions</u>.

4. He had human <u>experiences</u> and <u>needs</u>.

1. Jesus <u>limited</u> himself.

2. Jesus did not <u>lessen</u> himself.
   - This attitude is <u>humility</u>
     - As fully man, Jesus shows us that he <u>understands</u> our needs
     - As fully God, Jesus shows us that he can <u>meet</u> our needs

NOTES

KEY VERSES

One of the most effective ways to drive deeply into our lives the principles we are learning in this series is to memorize key Scriptures. For many, memorization is a new concept or one that has been difficult in the past. We encourage you to stretch yourself and try to memorize these four key verses. If possible, memorize these as a group and make them part of your group time. You may cut these apart and carry them in your wallet.

I have hidden your word in my heart that I might not sin against you.

Psalm 119:11 (NIV)

Session One

For in Christ all the fullness of the Deity lives in bodily form, and you have been given fullness in Christ, who is the head over every power and authority.

Colossians 2:9–10 (NIV)

Session Two

For by him all things were created: things in heaven and on earth, visible and invisible, whether thrones or powers or rulers or authorities; all things were created by him and for him.

Colossians 1:16 (NIV)

Session Three

In the beginning was the Word, and the Word was with God, and the Word was God.

John 1:1 (NIV)

Session Four

Your attitude should be same as that of Christ Jesus.

Philippians 2:5 (NIV)

NOTES

We value your thoughts about what you've just read.
Please email us at *zauthor@zondervan.com*.

The Purpose Driven® Life
A six-session video-based study for groups or individuals

Embark on a journey of discovery with this video-based study taught by Rick Warren. In it you will discover the answer to life's most fundamental question: "What on earth am I here for?"

And here's a clue to the answer: It's not about you . . . You were created by God and for God, and until you understand that, life will never make sense. It is only in God that we discover our origin, our identity, our meaning, our purpose, our significance, and our destiny."

Whether you experience this adventure with a small group or on your own, this six-session, video-based study will change your life.

DVD Study Guide: 978-0-310-27866-5
DVD: 978-0-310-27864-1

Be sure to combine this study with your reading of the best-selling book, *The Purpose Driven® Life*, to give you or your small group the opportunity to discuss the implications and applications of living the life God created you to live.

Hardcover, Jacketed: 978-0-310-20571-5
Softcover: 978-0-310-27699-9

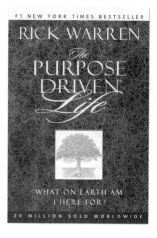

Pick up a copy today at your favorite bookstore!

ZONDERVAN®
.com

Foundations: 11 Core Truths to Build Your Life On

Taught by Tom Holladay and Kay Warren

Foundations is a series of 11 four-week video studies covering the most important, foundational doctrines of the Christian faith. Study topics include:

The Bible—This study focuses on where the Bible came from, why it can be trusted, and how it can change your life.

DVD Study Guide: 978-0-310-27670-8
DVD: 978-0-310-27669-2

God—This study focuses not just on facts about God, but on how to know God himself in a more powerful and personal way.

DVD Study Guide: 978-0-310-27672-2
DVD: 978-0-310-27671-5

Jesus—As we look at what the Bible says about the person of Christ, we do so as people who are developing a lifelong relationship with Jesus.

DVD Study Guide: 978-0-310-27674-6
DVD: 978-0-310-27673-9

The Holy Spirit—This study focuses on the person, the presence, and the power of the Holy Spirit, and how you can be filled with the Holy Spirit on a daily basis.

DVD Study Guide: 978-0-310-27676-0
DVD: 978-0-310-27675-3

Creation—Each of us was personally created by a loving God. This study does not shy away from the great scientific and theological arguments that surround the creation/evolution debate. However, you will find the goal of this study is deepening your awareness of God as your Creator.

DVD Study Guide: 978-0-310-27678-4
DVD: 978-0-310-27677-7

Pick up a copy today at your favorite bookstore!

ZONDERVAN®
.com

Salvation—This study focuses on God's solution to man's need for salvation, what Jesus Christ did for us on the cross, and the assurance and security of God's love and provision for eternity.

DVD Study Guide: 978-0-310-27682-1
DVD: 978-0-310-27679-1

Sanctification—This study focuses on the two natures of the Christian. We'll see the difference between grace and law, and how these two things work in our lives.

DVD Study Guide: 978-0-310-27684-5
DVD: 978-0-310-27683-8

Good and Evil—Why do bad things happen to good people? Through this study we'll see how and why God continues to allow evil to exist. The ultimate goal is to build up our faith and relationship with God as we wrestle with these difficult questions.

DVD Study Guide: 978-0-310-27687-6
DVD: 978-0-310-27686-9

The Afterlife—The Bible does not answer all the questions we have about what happens to us after we die; however, this study deals with what the Bible does tell us. This important study gives us hope and helps us move from a focus on the here and now to a focus on eternity.

DVD Study Guide: 978-0-310-27689-0
DVD: 978-0-310-27688-3

The Church—This study focuses on the birth of the church, the nature of the church, and the mission of the church.

DVD Study Guide: 978-0-310-27692-0
DVD: 978-0-310-27691-3

The Second Coming—This study addresses both the hope and the uncertainties surrounding the second coming of Jesus Christ.

DVD Study Guide: 978-0-310-27695-1
DVD: 978-0-310-27693-7

Pick up a copy today at your favorite bookstore!

ZONDERVAN
.com

Wide Angle:
Framing Your Worldview

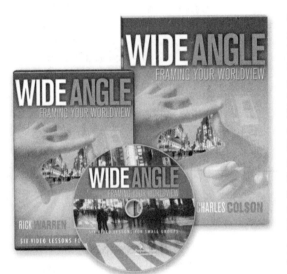

Christianity is much more than a religion. It is a worldview—a way of seeing all of life and the world around you. Your worldview impacts virtually every decision you make in life: moral decisions, relational decisions, financial decisions— everything. How you see the world determines how you face the world.

In this brand new study, Rick Warren and Chuck Colson discuss such key issues as moral relativism, tolerance, terrorism, creationism vs. Darwinism, sin and suffering. They explore in depth the Christian worldview as it relates to the most important questions in life:

- Why does it matter what I believe?

- How do I know what's true?

- Where do I come from?

- Why is the world so messed up?

- Is there a solution?

- What is my purpose in life?

This study is as deep as it is wide, addressing vitally important topics for every follower of Christ.

Rick Warren   *Chuck Colson*

DVD Study Guide: 978-1-4228-0083-6
DVD: 978-1-4228-0082-9

The Way of a Worshiper

The pursuit of God is the chase of a lifetime—in fact, it's been going on since the day you were born. The question is: Have you been the hunter or the prey?

This small group study is not about music. It's not even about going to church. It's about living your life as an offering of worship to God. It's about tapping into the source of power to live the Christian life. And it's about discovering the secret to friendship with God.

In these four video sessions, Buddy Owens helps you unpack the meaning of worship. Through his very practical, engaging, and at times surprising insights, Buddy shares truths from Scripture and from life that will help you understand in a new and deeper way just what it means to be a worshiper.

God is looking for worshipers. His invitation to friendship is open and genuine. Will you take him up on his offer? Will you give yourself to him in worship? Then come walk *The Way of a Worshiper* and discover the secret to friendship with God.

DVD Study Guide: 978-1-4228-0096-6
DVD: 978-1-4228-0095-9

THE WAY of a WORSHIPER

Your study of this material will be greatly enhanced by reading the book, *The Way of a Worshiper: Discover the Secret to Friendship with God.*

Celebrate Recovery, Updated Curriculum Kit

This kit will provide your church with the tools necessary to start a successful Celebrate Recovery program. *Kit includes:*

- Introductory Guide for Leaders DVD
- Leader's Guide
- 4 Participant's Guides (one of each guide)
- CD-ROM with 25 lessons
- CD-ROM with sermon transcripts
- 4-volume audio CD sermon series

Curriculum Kit: 978-0-310-26847-5

Participant's Guide 4-pack

The Celebrate Recovery Participant's Guide 4-pack is a convenient resource when you're just getting started or if you need replacement guides for your program.

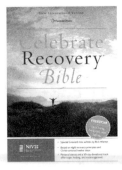

Celebrate Recovery Bible

With features based on eight principles Jesus voiced in his Sermon on the Mount, the new Celebrate Recovery bible offers hope, encouragement, and empowerment for those struggling with the circumstances of their livesand the habits they are trying to control.

Hardcover: 978-0-310-92849-2
Softcover: 978-0-310-93810-1

Pick up a copy today at your favorite bookstore!

ZONDERVAN®
.com

Stepping Out of Denial into God's Grace

Participant's Guide 1 introduces the eight principles of recovery based on Jesus' words in the Beatitudes, and focuses on principles 1–3. Participants learn about denial, hope, sanity, and more.

Getting Right with God, Yourself, and Others

Participant's Guide 3 covers principles 5–7 based on Jesus' words in the Beatitudes. With courage and support from their fellow participants, people seeking recovery will find victory, forgiveness, and grace.

Taking an Honest and Spiritual Inventory

Participant's Guide 2 focuses on the fourth principle based on Jesus' words in the Beatitudes and builds on the Scripture, *"Happy are the pure in heart."* (Matthew 5:8) The participant will learn an invaluable principle for recovery and also take an in-depth spiritual inventory.

Growing in Christ While Helping Others

Participant's Guide 4 walks through the final steps of the eight recovery principles based on Jesus' words in the Beatitudes. In this final phase, participants learn to move forward in newfound freedom in Christ, learning how to give back to others. There's even a practical lesson called "Seven reasons we get stuck in our recoveries."

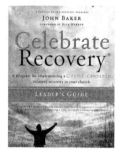

Leader's Guide

The Celebrate Recovery Leader's Guide gives you everything you need to facilitate your preparation time. Virtually walking you through every meeting, the Leader's Guide is a must-have for every leader on your Celebrate Recovery ministry team.

Pick up a copy today at your favorite bookstore!

Managing Our Finances God's Way

Did you know that there are over 2,350 verses in the Bible about money? Did you know that nearly half of Jesus' parables are about possessions? The Bible is packed with wise counsel about your financial life. In fact, Jesus had more to say about money than about heaven and hell combined.

Introducing a new video-based small group study that will inspire you to live debt free! Created by Saddleback Church and Crown Financial Ministries, learn what the Bible has to say about our finances from Rick Warren, Chip Ingram, Ron Blue, Howard Dayton, and Chuck Bentley as they address important topics like:

- God's Solution to Debt
- Saving and Investing
- Plan Your Spending
- Giving as an Act of Worship
- Enjoy What God Has Given You

Study includes:

- DVD with seven 20-minute lessons

- Workbook with seven lessons

- Resource CD with digital version of all worksheets that perform calculations automatically

- Contact information for help with answering questions

- Resources for keeping financial plans on track and making them lifelong habits

NOTE: PARTICIPANTS DO NOT SHARE PERSONAL FINANCIAL INFORMATION WITH EACH OTHER.

DVD Study Guide: 978-1-4228-0083-6
DVD: 978-1-4228-0082-9